Classic
Brainteasers

Martin Gardner
Illustrated by Jeff Sinclair

Sterling Publishing Co., Inc. New York

Library of Congress Cataloging-in-Publication Data

Gardner, Martin, 1914–
    Classic brainteasers / Martin Gardner ; illustrated by Jeff
Sinclair.
        p.   cm.
    Includes index.
    ISBN 0-8069-1260-X
    1. Puzzles—Juvenile literature.   [1. Puzzles.]   I. Sinclair,
Jeff, ill.   II. Title.
GV1493.G335   1994
793.73—dc20   94-17524
                                                                CIP
                                                                AC

10   9   8   7   6   5   4   3   2   1

Published 1994 by Sterling Publishing Company, Inc.
387 Park Avenue South, New York, N.Y. 10016
© 1994 by Wood's End, Inc.
Some of the puzzles in this volume appeared in
slightly different form in *The Arrow Book of
Brainteasers* by Martin Gardner
Distributed in Canada by Sterling Publishing
% Canadian Manda Group, P.O. Box 920, Station U
Toronto, Ontario, Canada M8Z 5P9
Distributed in Great Britain and Europe by Cassell PLC
Villiers House, 41/47 Strand, London WC2N 5JE, England
Distributed in Australia by Capricorn Link Ltd.
P.O. Box 665, Lane Cove, NSW 2066
Manufactured in the United States of America
All rights reserved

Sterling ISBN 0-8069-1260-X

Contents

1. Warming Up

A Wrong Spell

The wizard is doing his best to turn the prince into a frog by pronouncing the magic word. Nothing happens. Can you tell why his spell is not working?

Answer on page 82.

The Great Shoot-Out

Chester Chimp and Roger Rattlesnake are about to have a gunfight on the main street of Tombstone. Who do you think will win the shoot-out?

Answer on page 82.

A Secret Message

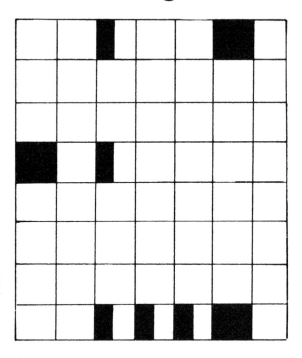

Shown above is a hidden greeting from me to you.
Can you decipher it?

Answer on page 82.

Nose Versus Feet

TEACHER: Our nose was made to smell with and our
feet were made to run with.

TOMMY: I must be made all wrong then, because my
nose _____ and my feet _____.

Can you think of the two missing words?

Answer on page 82.

Hidden Beasts and Insects

Hidden in the name of each living thing pictured here is the name of a *different* living thing. For example, concealed in the name "fox" is the word "ox." Can you find the animals hidden in the other names?

Answers on page 82.

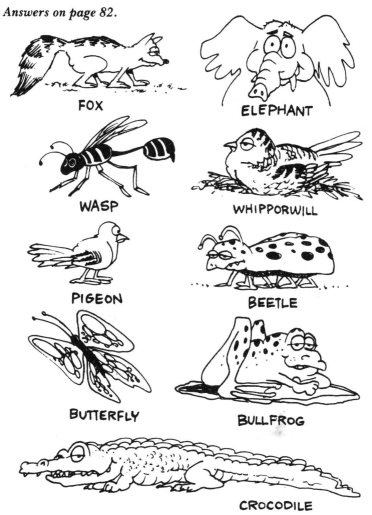

FOX

ELEPHANT

WASP

WHIPPORWILL

PIGEON

BEETLE

BUTTERFLY

BULLFROG

CROCODILE

Fat Bats and Other Mixed-Up Beasts

Each picture on these pages shows an animal that can be described by two words that rhyme. For example, the first picture is a fat bat, the second is a cryin' lion. How many of the others can you describe the same way?

Answers on page 82.

11

Silly Pictures

At first these drawings won't look like anything, just funny designs. But study them carefully. Suddenly you'll see them in a different way and the pictures will be clear to you. The poem below each drawing describes the scene. You fill in the missing words.

1. An _____ often
      Passes through
   A cloud that's floating
      In the blue.

2. An _____
      Named Happy Jack
   Likes to sunbathe
      On his back.

3. On the beach
      Miss Five-by-five
   Loves to do
      A fancy _____.

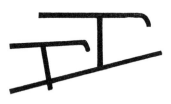

4. A _____ going
      Down a hill
   Turned a curve
      And took a spill.

Answers on page 82.

2. Word for Word

Wacky Wordles

Each word or group of words on these pages is printed so that it stands for a familiar phrase. For example, the first one means "A sock in the eye." Now see if you can guess the others!

① O 1 S O C K	② PANTS PANTS	③ TIRE
④ YOUR HAT KEEP IT	⑤ RANGER	⑥ SAFE FIRST

⑦ G R ROSIE i N

⑧ ENGAGE MENT

⑨ F R I E N D S STANDING MISS F R I E N D S

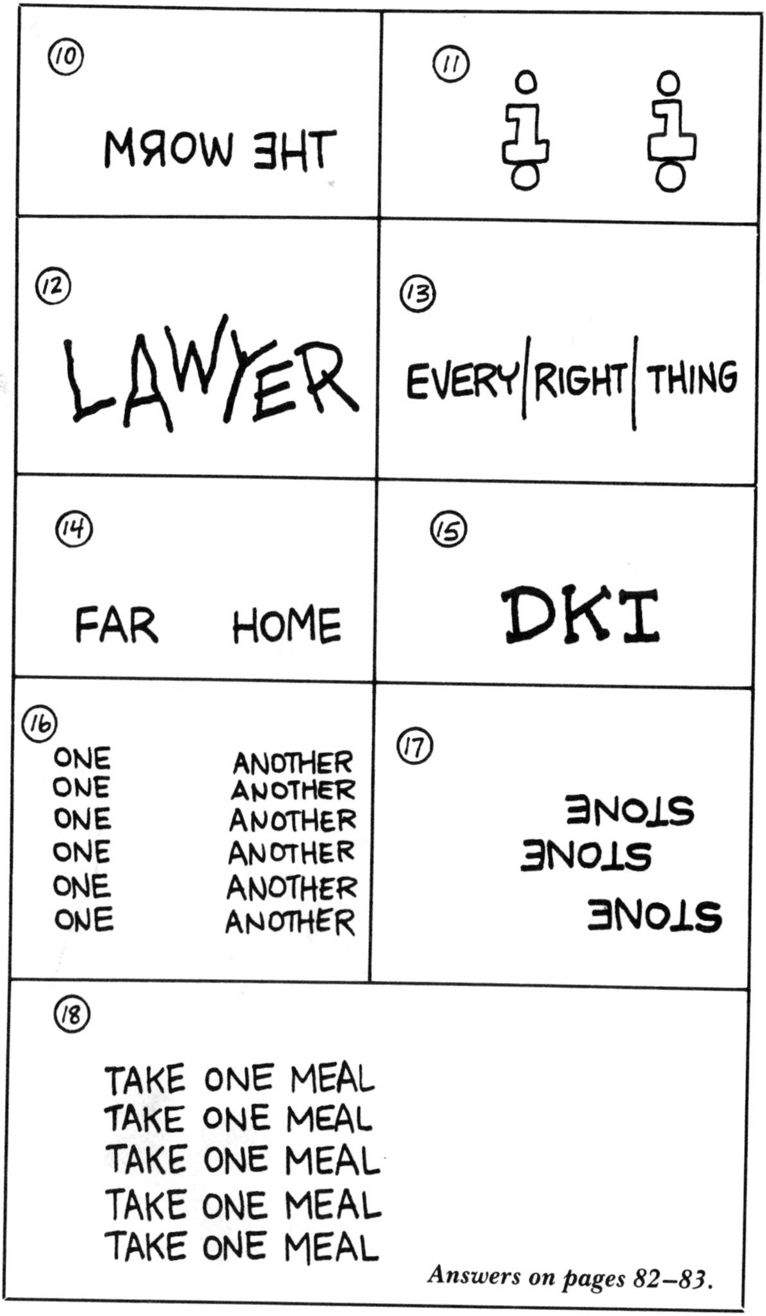

⑩

MᴚOW ƎHT

⑪

⑫

LAWYER

⑬

EVERY|RIGHT|THING

⑭

FAR   HOME

⑮

DKI

⑯

ONE   ANOTHER
ONE   ANOTHER
ONE   ANOTHER
ONE   ANOTHER
ONE   ANOTHER
ONE   ANOTHER

⑰

ƎИOTꙄ
ƎИOTꙄ
ƎИOTꙄ

⑱

TAKE ONE MEAL
TAKE ONE MEAL
TAKE ONE MEAL
TAKE ONE MEAL
TAKE ONE MEAL

Answers on pages 82–83.

15

Shifty Letters

Copy the squares shown directly above and then see if you can arrange them in line to spell the name of an animal.

Answer on page 83.

The Mysterious License

When Mr. Ollie Lee bought a new car, he asked for a license plate (marker) with the number 337 31770. Here's a picture of it. Can you figure out why he wanted these figures on it?

Answer on page 83.

Wilbur's Word

SNOWING

When Wilbur woke up and looked outside, it was snowing. The window was so misty that he could write "snowing" on it with his finger. Just for fun he rubbed out the letter "n" which left the word "sowing." Then he rubbed out another letter, and again it left a word.

He kept doing this. Every time he took away a letter, it left a word. Finally, only one letter was left and that was a word, too! How did Wilbur erase the letters?

Answer on page 83.

Hidden Proverb

A humorous twist on an old proverb is hidden in this border. See if you can read it by starting at the right letter, then taking every other letter as you go twice around the border.

Answer on page 83.

The Puzzling Grocer

This grocer likes to use signs that puzzle his customers. For example, the first sign means that he has peas for sale.

Can you figure out the other signs? Each one contains the hidden name of something else the grocer sells.

Answers on page 83.

The Hidden Names

This boy and girl have written some numbers on the blackboard. Can you guess their names?

Answers on page 83.

3. Look Sharp!

1. Odds Bodkins!

What's Wrong with These Pictures?

2. Videos

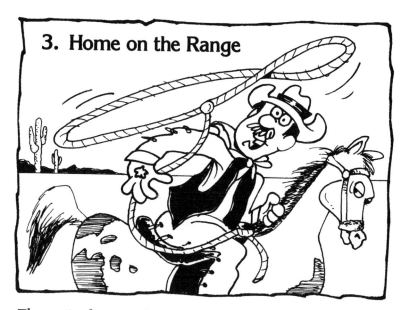

3. Home on the Range

The artist has made a serious error somewhere in each one of these pictures. Can you find the errors?

4. Fun in the Sun

Answers on page 84.

The Alphabet Zoo

Nine well-known animals can be spelled with the letters shown above. Start with any letter, then move along a black line, in any direction, to the next letter. Can you spell all the animals?

Answers on page 84.

The Careless Sign Painter

The sign painter made a careless mistake on his sign. See if you can correct his error by changing one of the letters.

Answer on page 84.

What Letter?

The three mysterious black shapes represent a letter of the alphabet. Can you guess the letter?

Answer on page 84.

Jane's Patchwork Quilt

When Jane sewed this patchwork quilt, she cleverly worked into it her own name and the names of all her girlfriends. The dotted line shows how to spell J-A-N-E by going from letter to adjoining letter. See if you can spell at least ten other girls' names in the same manner. You can spell up, down, sideways, or diagonally.

Answers on page 84.

Find the Missing Thief

The map you see below shows the street corners where four policemen are standing. A thief is hidden at one of the numbered intersections where he can't be seen by any one of the policemen. At which intersection can the thief be found?

Answer on page 84.

Find Charley's Car

Charley drove to town alone. After parking his car, he closed all its windows, got out and locked its doors, and then put a quarter in the parking meter. Which one of the five cars in the picture is Charley's?

Answer on page 84.

Napoleon at Home

Look carefully at this picture of Napoleon Bonaparte spending a quiet afternoon at home.

See if you can find ten things that did not exist in Napoleon's day.

Answers on page 84.

A Sheer Mistake

The artist made a mistake when he drew these scissors. Can you figure out what is wrong?

Answer on page 84.

Open-and-Shut Case

Mrs. Higgenbotham has opened the shutters to let in fresh air through the window. The artist has made a curious mistake. Can you spot it?

Answer on page 85.

Two Customers

A person who was unable to hear entered a stationery store to buy a wall pencil sharpener. To make the clerk understand what he wanted, he poked a finger into his left ear and then made a grinding motion around his other ear with his fist. The clerk understood at once.

A man who was unable to see now entered the store. How did he make the clerk understand that he wanted to buy a pair of scissors?

Answer on page 85.

The Pistol Duel

A century ago, two Frenchmen, Alphonse and Gaston, fought a duel with pistols. Each put a bullet through his opponent's head, yet neither Alphonse nor Gaston died. How could this be?

Answer on page 85.

Name the Product

CUSTOMER: How much is one?
CLERK: Thirty cents.
CUSTOMER: I'll take fourteen.
CLERK: Sixty cents.
CUSTOMER: I'll take a hundred and forty-four.
CLERK: That will be ninety cents.
What on earth is the customer buying?

Answer on page 85.

The Stolen Lugs

Mr. Green has removed a flat tire and is putting on the spare. He doesn't know that a squirrel is stealing the four lugs (nuts) that hold the tire to the axle. After finding the lugs missing, how does Mr. Green manage to attach his spare tire and drive to the nearest service station where he can obtain four more lugs?

Answer on page 85.

Donald Gets His Roller Blades

Donald lived with his parents and an older sister in a one-story brick house on the end of Main Street. One afternoon the doorbell rang. Donald opened the door. It was his friend Tommy, who lived across the street.

"Let's go skating," said Tommy.

"Okay," Donald said. "Wait there until I get my roller blades."

Donald ran quickly up the stairs. He got his skates from under the bed in his room on the second floor. Then he ran outside and put them on. He and Tommy spent the rest of the afternoon skating.

What's wrong with this story?

Answer on page 85.

Who Reads Faster?

If it takes Willie 80 minutes to read a short story, and it takes his sister an hour and ten minutes to read the same story, who is the faster reader?

Answer on page 85.

Ripping Good Puzzle

If you were to tear pages 8, 9, 48, 53 and 54 out of this book, how many separate sheets of paper would you rip out?

Answer on page 85.

A Knotty Problem

Can you figure out a way to hold a piece of rope or string, one end in each hand, and tie a knot in the string without letting go of either end?

Answer on page 85.

Find the Missing Word

See if you can put the right letters in the blank squares above so that each vertical column is a three-letter word, and the center horizontal row spells the name of a familiar sea animal. *Hint:* The pictures on the page will help you.

Answer on page 85.

Cops
and Robbers

To play this game, you need two coins of different sizes. The larger one represents the robber. Put it on the thief's picture.

The smaller coin is the policeman. Put it on the cop's picture. He is rushing out of the police station to catch the robber.

One player moves the smaller coin and the other moves the larger one.

Here are the simple rules:

1. The policeman always moves first. After that, players move in turns.
2. Each move is one block only, in any direction.
3. The policeman tries to catch the thief. This is accomplished by moving the smaller coin so that it lands on top of the larger one.
4. The thief tries to keep from getting caught. If he isn't captured in 50 of the policeman's moves, then *he* wins.

Hint: There is a secret way to catch the thief! If the cop knows it, he can catch the robber every time. But if he doesn't, the thief will never be caught.

Try playing the game for a while with a friend. If neither of you discovers the secret, turn to page 86, where the trick is explained.

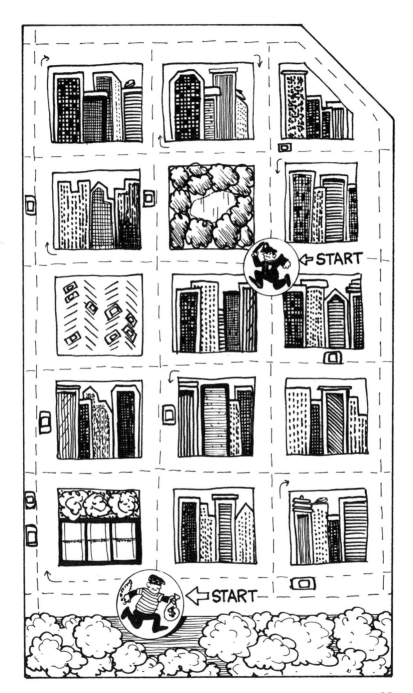

START

START

We Predict!

1. Write down the name of a country starting with D.
2. Write down the name of an animal starting with the second letter in the country's name.
3. Write down the color of the animal.
4. Write down the name of an animal starting with the *last* letter of the country's name.
5. Write down the name of a fruit starting with the last letter in the name of the animal you chose for the fourth step.

Now to the answer section. We'll give our prediction of the five words you have written!

Answers on page 86.

5. Teasers

Professor Egghead's PROVERBS

Professor J. Fortescue Egghead likes to use big words and complicated sentences. Here is how the professor would say eight well-known proverbs. See how many you can recognize, and then check the answers on page 86.

1 A rotating fragment of mineral collects no bryophytic plants.

2 *Exercise your visual faculties prior to executing a jump.*

3 UNDER NO CIRCUMSTANCES COMPUTE THE NUMBER OF YOUR BARNYARD FOWL PREVIOUS TO THEIR INCUBATION.

4 An excess of individuals skilled in the preparation of edibles impairs the quality of thin soup.

 5 A FEATHERED BIPED IN THE TERMINAL PART OF THE ARM EQUALS IN VALUE A PAIR OF FEATHERED BIPEDS IN DENSELY BRANCHED SHRUBBERY.

 6 A RECENTLY PURCHASED IMPLEMENT FOR BRUSHING AWAY FLOOR DIRT INVARIABLY EFFACES THE DIRT MOST EFFICIENTLY.

 7 A timorous heart at no time succeeds in acquiring the beautiful damsel.

 8 EVERYTHING IS LEGITIMATE IN MATTERS PERTAINING TO ARDENT AFFECTION AND ARMED CONFLICT BETWEEN NATIONS.

Answers on page 86.

Elvira's Jeans

After putting on a new pair of jeans, Elvira pushed her right hand all the way down into the left pocket of the pants, and pushed her left hand all the way down in her right pocket. How did she manage that?

Answer on page 86.

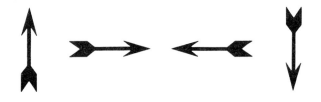

Name the Word

The symbols above stand for a familiar four-letter word. What word?

Answer on page 86.

A Burglary

The Johnsons have just reported a robbery. All the wife's jewels are missing.

"You'll want to check inside for fingerprints," Mr. Johnson said to the policeman.

"That won't be necessary," the policeman replied. "There's been no burglary."

What made the policeman so sure?

Answer on page 86.

The Amazing Computer

A store has on sale a computer and word processor small enough to fit in your pocket. It can add, multiply, subtract, divide, and write in all languages. A delete device will correct any error. No electricity is required to operate it. The price? Only a few cents! How can the store make a profit by selling it so cheap?

Answer on page 87.

Pat, the Goalie

Pat, the goalie on Central High's soccer team, said: "I'm the only player on the team who has a brother who can say truthfully that his father is the only man in town who doesn't have a son who goes to Central High."

This seems impossible. Can you explain?

Answer on page 87.

Mrs. Perkins' Pets

All of Mrs. Perkins' pets are dogs except one, and all her pets are cats except one. How many cats and dogs does she have?

Answer on page 87.

The Three Paths

Can you draw a path from Mr. Smith to the computer store, another path from Mrs. Smith to the fitness studio, and a third path from Jimmy Smith to the ballgame—without having one path cross another?

Answer on page 87.

Lost in the Woods

3	2	4	2	8	4	4	8	5
2	8	1	7	8	6	7	6	4
6	5	6	4	6	1	2	9	6
6	1	3	5	8	3	2	4	5
4	9	8	4	☆	4	8	7	6
8	2	7	1	9	8	9	2	6
5	2	2	8	5	8	4	7	4
1	4	3	9	2	6	2	5	4
7	6	2	2	6	9	8	6	3

The star marks the spot on this square-shaped forest where you are lost. The broken line shows how to get to the edge by moving only on even-number squares. Can you find a path to the edge using only odd-number squares?

You may move up or down, left or right, or diagonally.

Answer on page 87.

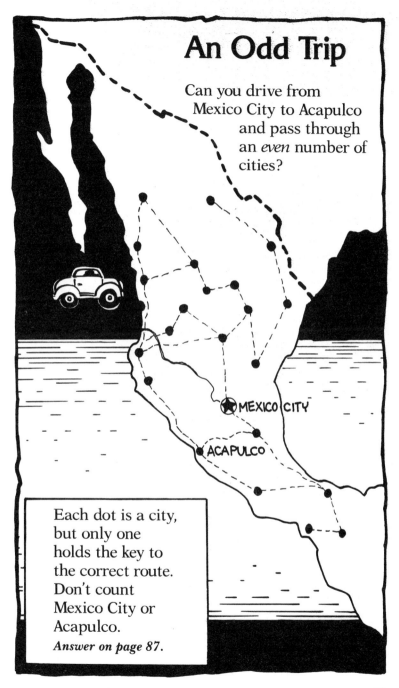

An Odd Trip

Can you drive from Mexico City to Acapulco and pass through an *even* number of cities?

Each dot is a city, but only one holds the key to the correct route. Don't count Mexico City or Acapulco.

Answer on page 87.

MEXICO CITY

ACAPULCO

Upside-Down Years

What year of this century is the same when its number is upside down? What year of the previous century is the same when inverted?

Answers on page 87.

Dog Bites Man

STRANGER *(to a farmer):* Does your dog bite?
FARMER: Nope.

The dog then bit the stranger on his leg. Yet the farmer told the truth. Explain!

Answer on page 87.

6. Science and Math Puzzles

Dots and Squares

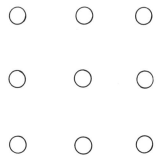

How many different squares are indicated by four spots that mark their corners?

Answer on page 87.

The Hindu Squares

How many different squares can you find in this picture? The answer looks easy, but it's harder than it seems. There may be more here than you think there are!

Answer on page 88.

Exploring the Moon

These astronauts are exploring a crater on the moon. Somewhere in the picture, the artist has made a scientific error.

First see if you can find it. Then check your guess with the answer on page 88.

Pepper or Salt?

This is Professor Piffle's latest invention—an automatic salt-and-pepper shaker. As you can imagine, he's very proud of it and uses it all the time to give his food flavor. Right now he's about to use it on one of his favorite dishes—hot soup. If he turns the crank in the direction of the arrow, will this amazing machine shake salt or pepper in his bowl of soup?

Answer on page 88.

Knots or Not?

If you pull on the ends of each rope shown above, two ropes will form knots and two won't. Can you pick out the two that will?

Answer on page 88.

The Triangular Cat

Here is an unusual cat made up entirely of triangles. How many different triangles can you find in the picture of this cat?

Answer on page 88.

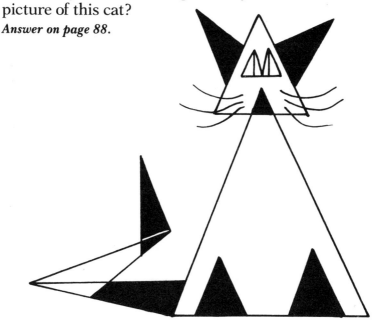

The Startled Astronomer

This amateur astronomer is examining a star that is twinkling between the horns of a new moon. Somewhere in this picture, too, the artist has made a glaring scientific error. Can you find it?

Answer on page 88.

The Puzzled Inventor

Professor Piffle is working on another mad invention with gear wheels. He is trying to figure out which way the wheel at the bottom will turn if he rotates the top wheel in the direction of the arrow.

What do you think?

Answer on page 88.

Lewis Carroll's SQUARES

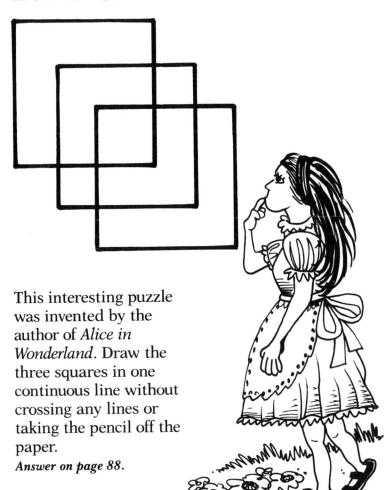

This interesting puzzle was invented by the author of *Alice in Wonderland*. Draw the three squares in one continuous line without crossing any lines or taking the pencil off the paper.

Answer on page 88.

7. Find the Mistakes

How many mistakes can you find in the pictures on the following pages?

Answers on page 89.

61

House & Back Yard

Answers on page 90.

Living Room

MISS TREE

Answers on page 90—91.

Landscape

Answers on page 91–92.

Crazy Timepiece

The artist has made exactly seven mistakes in this picture. Can you find all of them?

Answers on page 92.

8. Logic Puzzles

How Comes

1. Jones was caught stealing 27 times in one year, yet he was never arrested. How come?

2. A truck driver went three blocks the wrong way down a one-way street without breaking the law. How come?

3. A boy and girl are standing on the same sheet of newspaper, yet it is impossible for them to kiss. How come?

4. Not a single parent objected when the teacher spanked every child in the class. How come?

5. Thirty people died in a plane crash, but not a single survivor was buried. How come?

6. A cowboy rode into Dodge City on Friday, stayed two days, then rode out of town on Friday. How come?

7. A man tossed a soccer ball ten feet. It stopped in midair, reversed direction and came back to him. How come?

8. 96 is not 69 upside down. How come?

9. There are only two Rs in "Robert Richardson." How come?

10. A dog trotted all the way across a lake without sinking in the water. How come?

11. A prizefighter was unconscious seven times during the same week, yet he was never ill or injured or knocked out in a fight. How come?

12. A person living in Oklahoma can't be buried in Texas. How come?

13. A snooper was able to see right through the brick wall of a house. How come?

14. A lady took her poodle for a walk. The dog did not walk ahead of her, behind her, or on one side. How come?

15. A man married 57 women. None died, and he was never divorced, yet he was one of the most admired men in town. How come?

16. A man drove all the way from Montreal to Vancouver without knowing he had a flat tire. How come?

Answers on page 92–93.

Slice the Pie

Mrs. Murphy is trying to figure out how she can cut her apple pie with four straight cuts and make the largest number of pieces. What is the largest number you can get with four cuts?

Answer on page 93.

The Clever Postman

When the postman arrived at the Smith home to deliver mail through a slot in the front door, he was surprised to find the Smiths had acquired a vicious dog. The dog was fastened to a tree by a chain just long enough to reach the front door.

The dog growled and bared its teeth. How did the clever postman outwit the dog and reach the door safely?

Answer on page 93.

Name the Men

Mr. Cook, Mr. Sailor and Mr. Carpenter met on the street one afternoon.

"Isn't it funny," said Mr. Cook to the others, "that not one of us has a profession that is the same as our names?"

"That's true," agreed the man who was the carpenter.

Can you now give the correct last name of each man shown in the above picture?

Answer on page 93.

Hint: Since Mr. Cook is talking to the carpenter, he cannot be the carpenter.

The Colored Socks

Ten red socks and ten green socks are all mixed up in a drawer. They are exactly alike except for color. If you close your eyes, then open the drawer and take out some socks without looking at them, what is the smallest number you can take out and still be absolutely sure that you have a pair of socks that match?

Answer on page 93.

The Fourth Child

Mary's mother, Mrs. Jones, had exactly four children. The oldest, a boy, she named North. The next oldest, a girl, she named South. The third child, a boy, she named East. The youngest child was another girl. What was her first name?

Answer on page 93.

The Clever Prisoner

KING: One box contains a white marble, the other box contains a black marble. You may select either box. If you choose the white marble, you go free. If you choose the black marble, you will be hanged."

The prisoner knew that the king was an evil man, and that each box contained a black marble. What did he do to escape death?

Answer on page 94.

The Smiths' Family Tree

This family tree shows Mr. and Mrs. Ebenezer Smith and their descendants for three generations. Francis Smith, the only member of the third generation, appears in the bottom row of great-grandchildren. Remember that only the male child carries on the family name when he gets married. Now see if you know which one of the children is Francis Smith.

Answer on page 94.

The Mysterious Tracks

Mr. Shamrock Jones, the great detective, is trying to figure out who or what made these odd-looking tracks that lead across the snow towards a woodshed on the farm. What is your guess?

Answer on page 94.

Where's the Tiger?

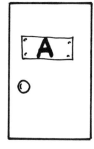 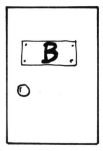 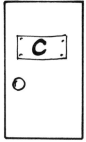 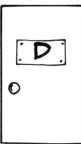

The tiger is in B or C.

The tiger is in A or D.

The tiger is here.

The tiger is not here.

This one isn't easy. A tiger is behind one of the four doors. Three of the statements below the doors are false. Where is the tiger?

Answer on page 94.

Name the Relation

"The father of this person," said the man as he pointed to a photograph in his hand, "is my father's son, yet I have no brothers and no sons."

What relation was the man to the person in the picture?

Answers on page 94.

Heads or Tails?

Someone gives you a coin. You flip it fifty times and each time it comes up heads. If you flip it once more, which is most likely, heads or tails?

Answer on page 94.

A Wrong Spell
The Wizard is pronouncing the magic word incorrectly. It is "Abracadabra," not "Abradacabra."

The Great Shoot-Out
Roger Rattlesnake will lose the gunfight because he has no hands with which to draw his gun.

A Secret Message
Tip the page forward so that you view the picture from a steep slant and you will see the greeting.

Nose Versus Feet
Tommy said, ". . . my nose runs and my feet smell."

Hidden Beasts and Insects
F[ox]; eleph[ant]; w[asp]; w[hippo]orwill; [pig]eon; [bee]tle; butter[fly]; [bull]frog; cro[cod]ile.

Fat Bats and Other Mixed-Up Beasts
Square bear.   Sick chick.
Half giraffe.   Full bull.
Girl squirrel.   Colossal fossil.
Mobster lobster.   Deep sheep.
Jolly polly.   Talkin' falcon.
Golfin' dolphin.   Cleaner hyena.
Kickin' chicken.   Frail whale.

Silly Pictures
1. Airplane.
2. Elephant.
3. Dive.
4. Skier.

Wacky Wordles
2. A pair of pants.
3. A flat tire.
4. Keep it under your hat.

5. The Lone Ranger.
6. Safe on first.
7. Ring around Rosie.
8. A broken engagement.
9. A small misunderstanding between friends.
10. The worm turned.
11. Dark circles under the eyes.
12. A crooked lawyer.
13. Right in the middle of everything.
14. Far away from home.
15. Mixed-up kid.
16. Six of one and half a dozen of another.
17. No stone is left unturned.
18. Take one before every meal.

Shifty Letters
Turning the W square upside down makes it an M, and turning the U square on the side makes it a C. The answer is CAMEL.

The Mysterious License
Turn the page upside down!

Wilbur's Word
Snowing, sowing, owing, wing, win, in, I.

Hidden Proverb
Start at the bottom corner on the left and then move counter-clockwise to spell "He who laughs last is the slowest."

The Puzzling Grocer
1. Peas 2. Cantaloupe 3. Tomatoes 4. Rice 5. Cookies 6. Cottage Cheese

The Hidden Names
Hold the page to a mirror!

What's Wrong with These Pictures?
1. The knight's sword is straight, but his scabbard is curved.
2. The TV set is not plugged in.
3. The rope is behind the cowboy's hand.
4. The acrobats' shadows are not in the correct position.

The Alphabet Zoo
Cat, dog, cow, horse, lion, tiger, pig, bat, hog.

The Careless Sign Painter
The sign should read "AGILE MONKEYS."

What Letter?
Rotate the page 90° clockwise, and you'll see a capital E.

Jane's Patchwork Quilt
The following girls' names can be spelled: Ann, Lulu, Diana, Diane, Lena, Dinah, Edna, Maud, Hannah, Jennie, Minnie, Anna, Mary, Nan, Nancy, Jane, Mae, and Judy.

Find the Missing Thief
The thief is standing at intersection Number 9.

Find Charley's Car
Charley's car is the one that has no open door, no open window, no passenger inside, and is parked by a meter. It's the second car from the top.

Napoleon at Home
TV set, electric lamp, telephone, car, airplane, picture of Lincoln, picture of the Statue of Liberty, package of potato chips, box of cleansing tissues, computer.

A Sheer Mistake
The scissors cannot close!

Open-and-Shut Case
Slats slant opposite ways on opposite sides of a shutter. In this picture, the slats slant the same way on both sides.

Two Customers
The man said to the clerk, "I want to buy a pair of scissors."

The Pistol Duel
Alphonse and Gaston did not duel each other.

Name the Product
The customer is buying house numbers.

The Stolen Lugs
Mr. Green removed one lug from each of the other three tires and used them to attach the spare. Three lugs will hold a tire firmly enough for a short drive.

Donald Gets His Roller Blades
Donald lived in a one-story house, so he couldn't have had a bedroom on the second floor.

Who Reads Faster?
Willie's sister is the faster reader. She finished the story in 70 minutes, which is ten minutes less than Willie's 80 minutes.

Ripping Good Puzzle
Four. Pages 53 and 54 are two sides of the same sheet.

A Knotty Problem
Cross your arms before you seize the ends of the string. Uncross your arms and it will tie a knot in the cord.

Find the Missing Word
The sea animal is OYSTER.

Cops and Robbers

In the upper right-hand corner of the picture, the streets form a triangular block. This enables the cop to catch the robber.

In order to catch the thief, the cop must first move *all the way around* this triangular block. Once this is done, he will find it simple to trap the robber in one of the three square corners.

But if the cop doesn't go around the triangle first, he'll never catch the thief.

Keep this secret all to yourself. Then you'll be able to beat your friends every time you play.

We Predict!

You wrote down: DENMARK, ELEPHANT, GREY, KANGAROO, and ORANGE.

Professor Egghead's PROVERBS

1. A rolling stone gathers no moss.
2. Look before you leap.
3. Never count your chickens before they hatch.
4. Too many cooks spoil the broth.
5. A bird in the hand is worth two in the bush.
6. A new broom sweeps clean.
7. Faint heart ne'er won fair lady.
8. All's fair in love and war.

Elvira's Jeans

She put the jeans on backwards.

Name the Word

The word is NEWS, the initial letters of North, East, West and South, the four directions in which the arrows are pointing.

A Burglary

When a window is broken from the outside by a thief, the glass is all over the *inside* of the room.

86

The Amazing Computer
The computer is a wooden pencil with an eraser.

Pat, the Goalie
Pat is a girl. Her brother has graduated from Central High.

Mrs. Perkins' Pets
Mrs. Perkins has one cat and one dog.

The Three Paths

Lost in the Woods
Find your way out by moving from the star to 3, 1, 7, 9, 5.

An Odd Trip
To solve the puzzle, all you have to do is be sure to pass *through* the city nearest the front wheel of the car.

Upside-Down Years
The invertible years are 1961 and 1881.

Dog Bites Man
The farmer told the truth, because it wasn't his dog.

Dots and Squares
There are six different squares.

The Hindu Squares
There are five small squares, five middle-sized squares, and one large one—11 in all.

Exploring the Moon
There are no clouds on the moon. Clouds are masses of water vapor floating in the atmosphere, but there is neither atmosphere nor water on the moon.

Pepper or Salt?
It will shake salt into the soup.

Knots or Not?
Ropes 1 and 2 will form knots when the ends are pulled.

The Triangular Cat
The cat is made up of 20 triangles.

The Startled Astronomer
It is not possible for a star to be inside a crescent moon. The crescent is simply an edge of the moon illuminated by the sun. The rest of the round moon is still there, only it is dark and you cannot see it against the dark sky. To be inside the crescent, a star would have to be between the moon and the earth, but no star is that close to us.

The Puzzled Inventor
The bottom wheel can't turn at all! The three wheels joined like a triangle would lock and refuse to rotate.

Lewis Carroll's SQUARES

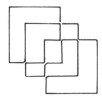

Barbershop

1. The image of the clock in the mirror should have the numbers reversed, but it doesn't.

2. The clock's minute hand in the mirror points straight up at 12, but the hour hand is halfway between 3 and 4.

3. The wall calendar for April has 31 days.

4. The sign on the window saying "BILL'S BARBERSHOP" is not reversed. It could not be read from outside.

5. "Wednesday" is spelled "Wendsday."

6. Outside the window, the back of the lady's handbag is missing.

7. The raindrops are upside down.

8. The blades of the scissors held by the barber can't close.

9. Each of the barber's hands has only three fingers and a thumb.

10. The barber's ear is upside down.

11. The barber chair has no handle for raising and lowering.

12. The customer has a moustache, but it is not reflected in the mirror.

13. The customer's solid color tie is striped in the mirror.

14. The customer is wearing glasses. (Glasses are always removed during a haircut.)

15. One lens of the customer's glasses is round, and the other is square.

16. The customer has different shoes on each foot.

17. On the floor, leaning against the wall, is an umbrella. It has its handle on the wrong end.

18. The cane next to the umbrella comes to a sharp point at the lower end.

19. On the street door, the knob and the hinges are on the same side.

20. The customer's jacket on the clothes rack has sleeves of different lengths.

21. And its buttons and button holes are on the wrong side.

House and Back Yard

1. The weathervane has East and West reversed.
2. The weathervane arrow shows wind blowing in one direction, while the smoke from the chimney is blowing the other way.
3. The man's shadow is not opposite the sun.
4. There is no other shadow in the picture.
5. A drop, dripping from the faucet, is upside down.
6. Water from the hose is making an impossible curve.
7. The hose is not connected to the house's faucet.
8. The birdhouse on top of the pole is floating an inch above the pole.
9. The sprinkler watering can has no holes.
10. One of the flower pots has no drainage hole in the bottom.
11. The dog on the lawn has its feet in impossible positions.
12. The dog has no ears.
13. The cat seems suspended in midair. It is not resting on any branch.
14. The cat has an extra long tail.
15. The handles on the casement windows are on the outside.
16. The bolt on the edge of the bottom part of the door is not lined up with the doorknob.
17. The bottom part of the door is too low to allow a person to enter.
18. There is no handle on the top part of the door.
19. One of the steps to the back door is too high.
20. The railing for the steps is too low.
21. The gutter on the roof slants away from the spout.

Living Room

1. The chandelier is not attached to the ceiling.
2. The shade on the lamp is upside down.
3. A bird cage hanging from the ceiling has wires so far apart the bird could fly out.

4. Mounted on the wall is a musket gun, but the trigger is backward.

5. A pencil is overhanging the table so far that it would fall off.

6. The table by the chair is missing a back leg.

7. One side of the book the man is reading is longer than the other.

8. The book's title is on the wrong side.

9. The word "mystery" on the book is misspelled.

10. The picture of Whistler's Mother over the fireplace shows her watching TV.

11. One of the pictures is hanging off-center in an impossible way.

12. The table has a folding leaf, but the hinges are on top of the join.

13. The chessboard is 6 × 8 squares instead of 8 × 8.

14. The window opens by lifting up, but there are hinges on one side.

15. There is an open gap in the woman's bead necklace.

16. The heels on the woman's shoes are of different heights.

17. The pitcher on the table has its handle on the side, not opposite the spout.

18. There is a porthole on the wall showing the ocean outside.

19. The piano has no black keys.

20. The top of the swivel stool is off-center from the post beneath it.

21. One of the small repeating patterns in the woman's chair is different from the others.

22. The window shade is all the way up. Its pull is off-center.

Landscape
1. One of the clouds is going *behind* the sun.

2. A crescent moon would be invisible in the sunlight.

3. The crescent moon should be pointing towards the sun.
4. The ends of the crescent moon never extend this far.
5. The rainbow in the distance is not opposite the sun.
6. The road sign is not connected to the post.
7. The turtle has three legs on one side.
8. The cow has the horns of a bull.
9. The rabbit has only one ear.
10. A swan in the lake has no reflection.
11. A rowboat on the edge of the lake has two oarlocks on the same side.
12. The blade of one oar is round, the other is rectangular.
13. Roses and tulips are growing on one bush.
14. The road has a wide crack.
15. Birds in the air are upside down.
16. The snake on the road has legs.
17. Pigs can't fly.
18. The outline of the tree shows all rounded leaves, but the individual leaves are all pointed.
19. It's only raining in one spot.
20. The tree has a hole in it.
21. The plane's position is impossible. A full-size plane would have to be *behind* the column of rain.
22. The airplane has only one wing.

Crazy Timepiece
1. Hours 7 and 8 are reversed. 2. With the minute hand at 12, the hour hand doesn't point between numbers. 3. 10 is in Roman numerals. 4. 3 is reversed. 5. 5 is at an angle. 6. There are four minutes between 5 and 6. 7. There are 6 minutes between 11 and 12.

How Comes
1. The man was a baseball player who stole bases.
2. The truck driver was on foot.
3. They were standing on opposite sides of a door.

4. The children were in an orphanage school.
5. Survivors are not dead.
6. Friday was the name of the cowboy's horse.
7. He tossed the soccer ball straight up in the air.
8. 96 upside down is still 96.
9. The other two r's in Robert Richardson are lower case.
10. The lake was frozen.
11. The prizefighter was asleep in bed seven times.
12. He isn't dead.
13. The snooper looked through a window.
14. The poodle walked on the other side.
15. The man was a minister.
16. It was his spare tire that was flat.

Slice the Pie

The Clever Postman

The postman ran around the tree in circles. The dog followed him until the chain wrapped around the trunk enough times to keep the dog away from the door. The dog was not smart enough to unwind the chain.

Name the Men

Mr. Cook couldn't be the cook, nor could he be the carpenter, because the carpenter replied to his question. So he must be the sailor. Mr. Carpenter can't be the carpenter or the sailor, so he must be the cook. This leaves Mr. Sailor, who must be the carpenter.

The Colored Socks

Three socks.

The Fourth Child

The child was named Mary.

The Clever Prisoner

The prisoner opened a box, concealed the marble in his fist, popped it into his mouth, and swallowed it. To determine its color, the other box had to be opened and, of course, it contained a black marble. In this way, the prisoner did not openly accuse the king of fraud, and his life was saved.

The Smiths' Family Tree

Spelled with an "i," Francis is always a boy's name. He is fourth from the left in the bottom row.

The Mysterious Tracks

The tracks were made by a man with a peg leg, pushing a wheelbarrow.

Where's the Tiger?

The tiger is behind Door D.

Name the Relation

The man is the father of the person in the photograph—his daughter!

Heads or Tails?

Heads is most likely. If a coin shows heads each time on fifty flips, it is surely a coin with heads on both sides.

About the Author

World-famous as the puzzlemaster who wrote the "Mathematical Games" column of *Scientific American* magazine for 25 years, Martin Gardner has also written close to 50 books, on such subjects as science (including a book that *Time* magazine called "by far the most lucid explanation of Einstein's theories"), mathematics, philosophy, religion, poetry, literary criticism (including *The Annotated Alice*, a classic examination of *Alice in Wonderland* that is still selling large numbers of copies now, more than 30 years after it was first published) and, of course, puzzles (out of 29 puzzle books for adults and children, only one is out of print!).

The son of an Oklahoma wildcat oil prospector, Gardner attended the University of Chicago, where he received a degree in philosophy. After graduation he worked on the *Tulsa* (Oklahoma) *Tribune*. He sold his first story to *Esquire*, published articles on logic and math in specialist magazines and became a contributing editor to *Humpty Dumpty's Magazine* before starting his legendary column.

Martin Gardner has had a lifelong passion for conjuring, and many of his original magic tricks have become classics among magicians.

Dubbed "The Magician of Math" by *Newsweek*, Martin Gardner, now retired, makes his home in North Carolina, where he continues to amaze his fans with more and more books, articles and ideas.

Index

PLEASE SHARE YOUR THOUGHTS
ON THIS BOOK:

COMMENTS: I really liked the book	COMMENTS: I+ really fricked my most.
COMMENTS: alot it was great Kim.N.	COMMENTS:
COMMENTS: I couldn't solve alot. I really stupid	COMMENTS:
COMMENTS:	COMMENTS:
COMMENTS:	COMMENTS:
COMMENTS:	COMMENTS: